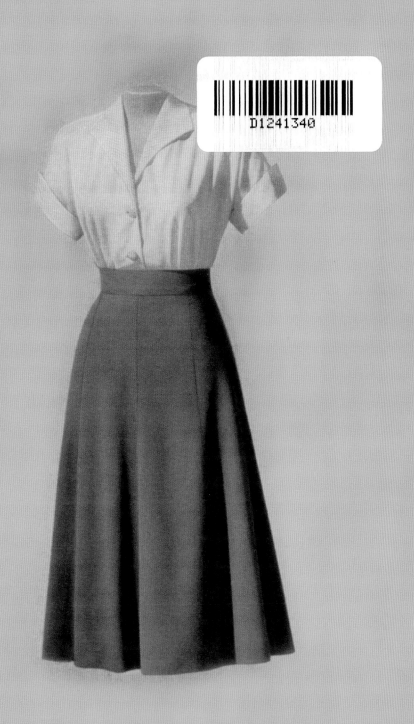

c

a

t

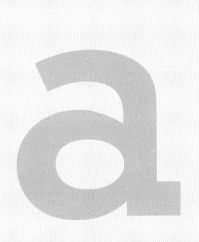

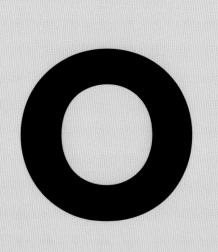

g

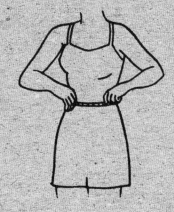

Conceived and Designed by Carin Goldberg

WITH AN INTRODUCTION BY DOROTHY TWINING GLOBUS

STEWART, TABORI & CHANG

NEW YORK

LOOKING
at an old mail-order
catalog from the fifties, one
is struck by the fact that life must have
been simpler when one volume could provide
all of the products necessary for daily life and a gen-
erous selection of less essential "luxuries." The index for
such a book runs to ten pages of six-point type. Clothing all
the family members, furnishing the home, caring for the
car, suggesting vacation activities from tents to outboard
motors, such catalogs offered solutions to one's every
need and desire......... For many decades, they were a primary
source of consumer goods for a great portion of the country.
In retrospect, they are powerful evocations of past eras.

Carin Goldberg, ever on the lookout for useful images,
acquired a winter 1951–1952 mail-order catalog at a local flea
market........... This densely packed tome of yellowing pages
became more than a visual resource as she focussed in on
the pristine presentation of the objects of daily life. Her very
personal selection of some sixty objects from this volume of
thousands of products prompts one to wonder about the
objects themselves, how they are presented, what they meant
then and now............... She is not attracted by the nostalgia
evoked by the visions of this past era. The images she has
chosen are pure forms, minimally decorative, juxtaposed to
suggest further associations and ideas. A whole page of
lady's slips, overlapping to maximize the number on the
page is a shopping medium............. A single one of these
garments, isolated from the rest, is a mysterious image,
sculptural and alluring even as it is unassuming.

As a graphic designer herself, Carin imagines the company
design department assembling the catalog. Even if this was
a tedious day job, they brought an unconscious aesthetic to
the process. Visual presentation was a challenge. As tiny
halftones, these objects had to entice and attract as they
competed with each other, crammed upon the pages.

They had to sell themselves without ever being
seen in real time............... The great effort that
went into the presentations can be seen
in the details: the careful arrangement of
the folds of garments, the modeling of the
forms, the backgrounds, the clarity of the
photography. That the designers got the most
out of the format becomes apparent when the
images are viewed at close range.

Extricated from their original context, these
images take on new significance and meaning.
By closely examining the individual pieces,
one comes to respect the strength of the
original renderings.................... The elemental
forms of prosaic objects and the painterly
treatment of undulating folds of light and
shadow are heightened by the visual effect of
the digital scans of the original half-tones.

The technical quality of the photographs holds up under the scrutiny of the new technology.................... The images have not been altered in any way aside from being placed within extended backgrounds............. One suspects that, despite the drudgery of assembling such catalogs, the artists labored with commitment to a strong work ethic..................... Season after season, they were conscientious and careful, creating these sales tools of the highest quality.

The conventions of the time dictated some of the representations............... Undergarments are discreetly presented without specific reference to those demure ladies who would buy them. The underpants are flattened out, the girdles only hint at curvature. The tension between proper and provocative, however, iş unavoidable. The sculptural forms of long-line brassieres float suggestively on the page........................ Were the photos airbrushed to clarify the conic contours? The slips are cinched in at the waist, a promise of slimness that also emphasizes the bust................. The very colors are evocative, pale flesh tones, delicate pinks and blues. Cheap thrills in less explicit days!

The pairings of the various images are suggestive, mysterious, surreal. They pay homage to Man Ray's chance encounter of a sewing machine and an umbrella on an ironing board......................... A basketball echoes the rounded cups of a brassiere, a story of contoured stitching. Vertical ribbing reinforces both woolly slipper socks and a gartered girdle. A utilitarian kitchen stool meets a stack of handkerchiefs....................... The patterns of perforations in three rubber girdles seem almost decorative beside an array of budding roses. A Magritte-like man's somber overcoat contrasts with a carefully folded scarf........ A light fixture and a truss are weirdly similar.

The mail-order catalog was a book of dreams and hopes, full of possibilities for changing and bettering life. These were flimsy, cheaply printed books, but they stayed around long after the season of issue and they provided all manner of secondary diversions. They made great reading material in idle moments. The brightly colored images were cut up and pasted into rainy day scrapbooks, the figures transformed into paper dolls, the pages used to paper walls of rooms. Decades later, such catalogs continue to entice with their offerings for life of times past as seen in the kinds of objects, the language of the texts, the style of graphic design. They are a far cry from the unending stream of glossy catalogs filling today's mailbox. Carin was seduced by a single issue. Even as she has studiously avoided nostalgia, she has shown the evocative power of these seemingly humble images.

Dorothy Twining Globus................. February 15, 2001, New York City

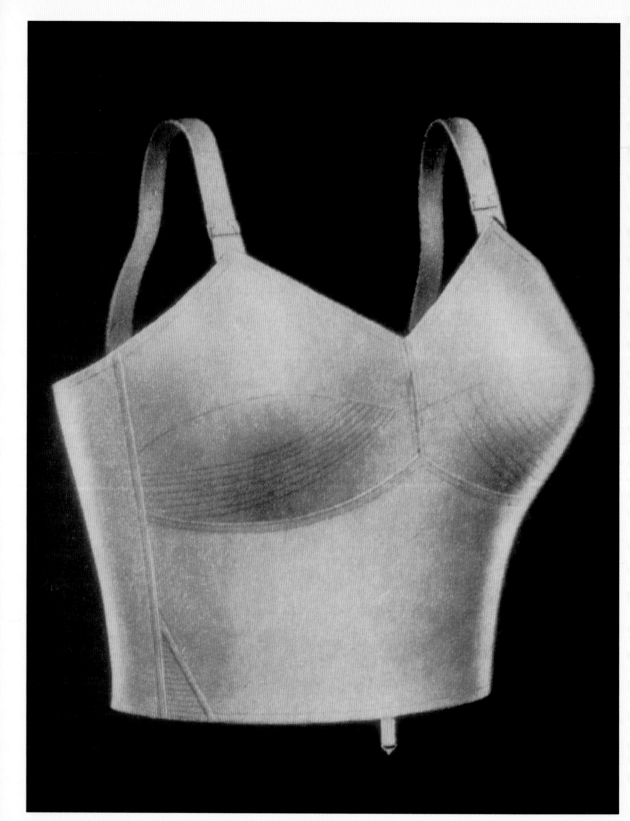

32 C 5294

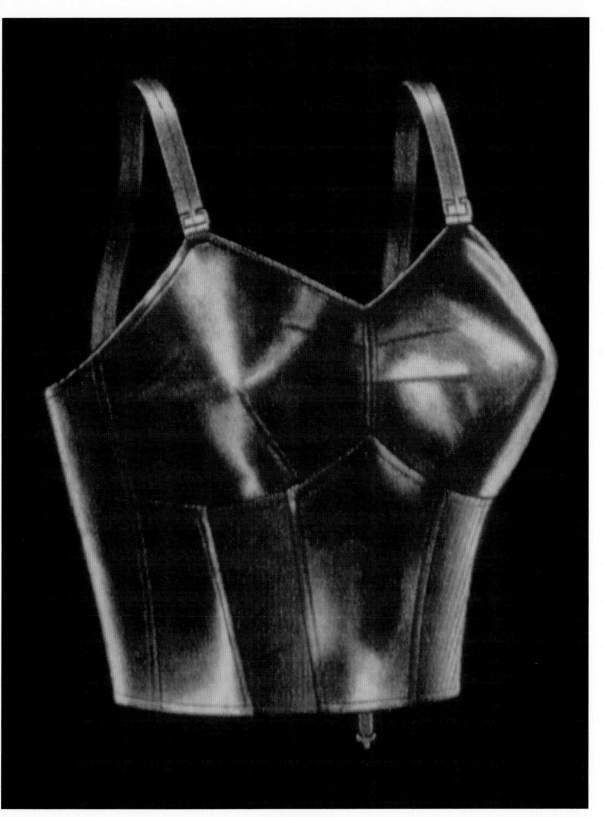

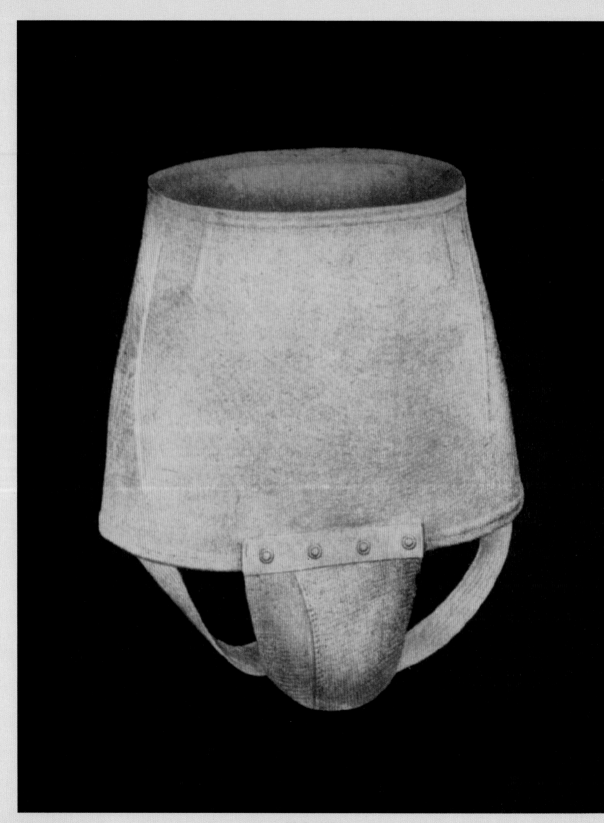

53 C 6675

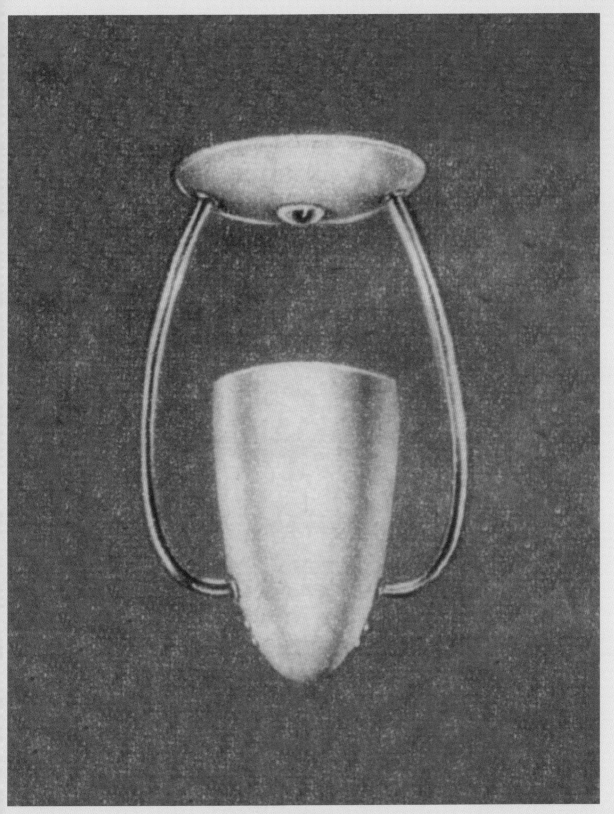

83 C 2525 L

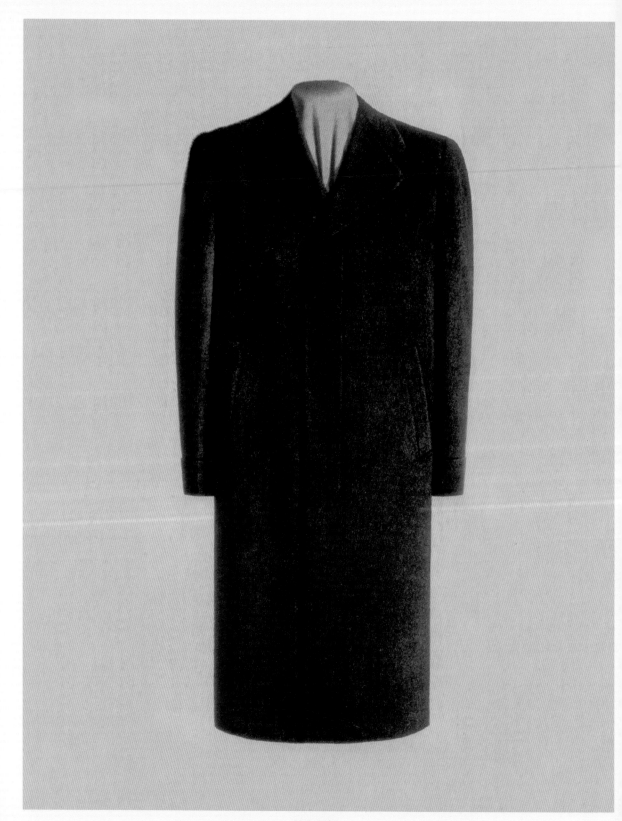

MC 4436

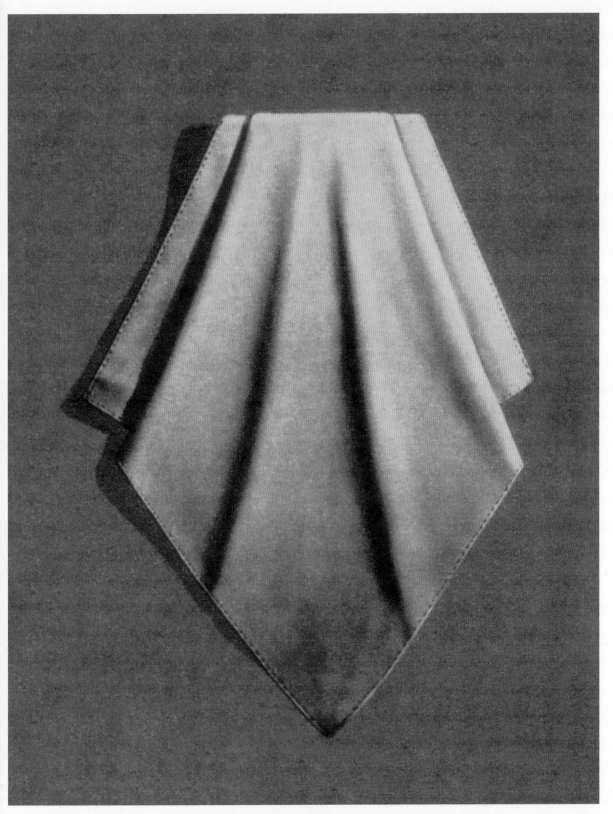

30 C 2707

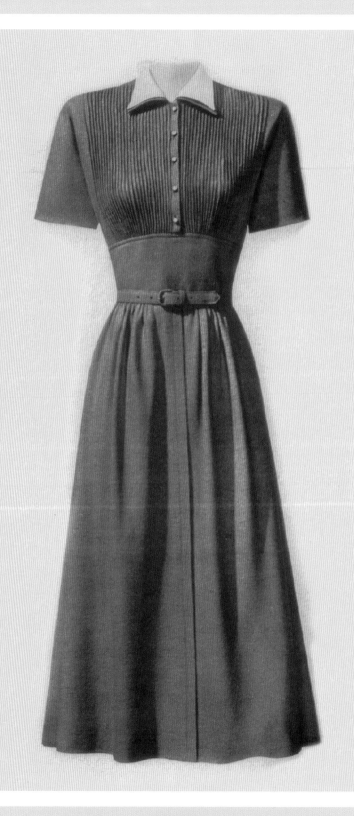

DC 8364

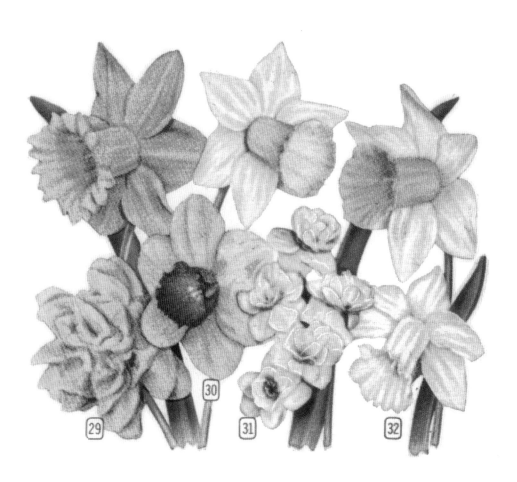

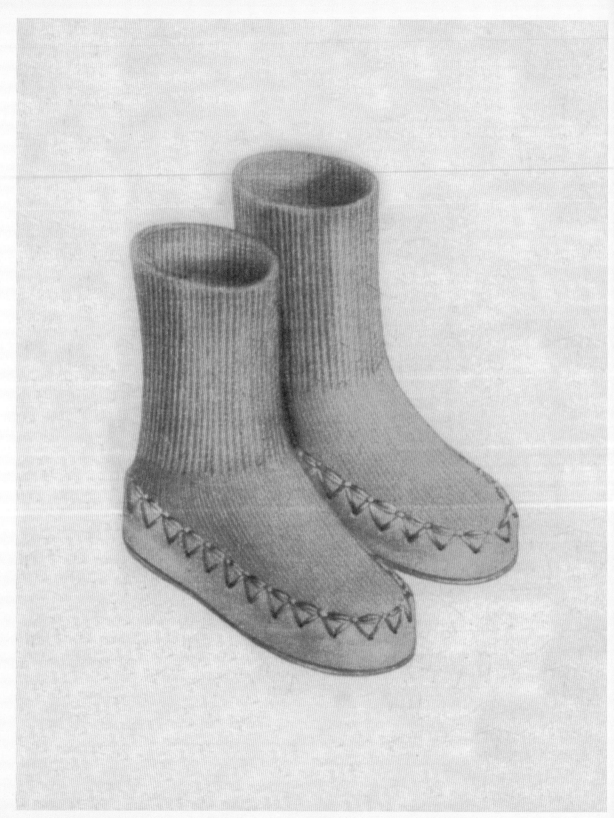

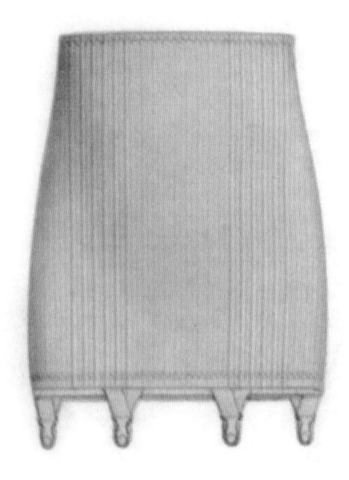

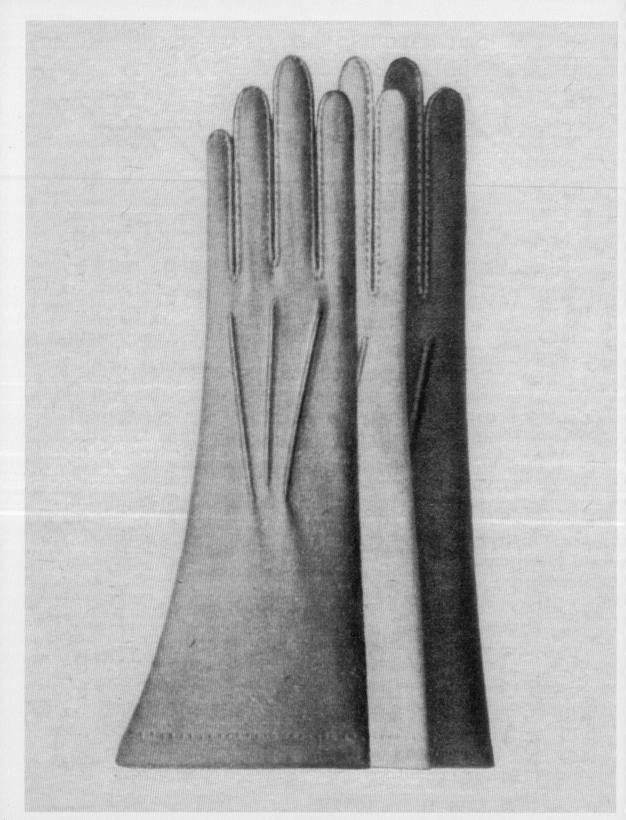

30 C 2111

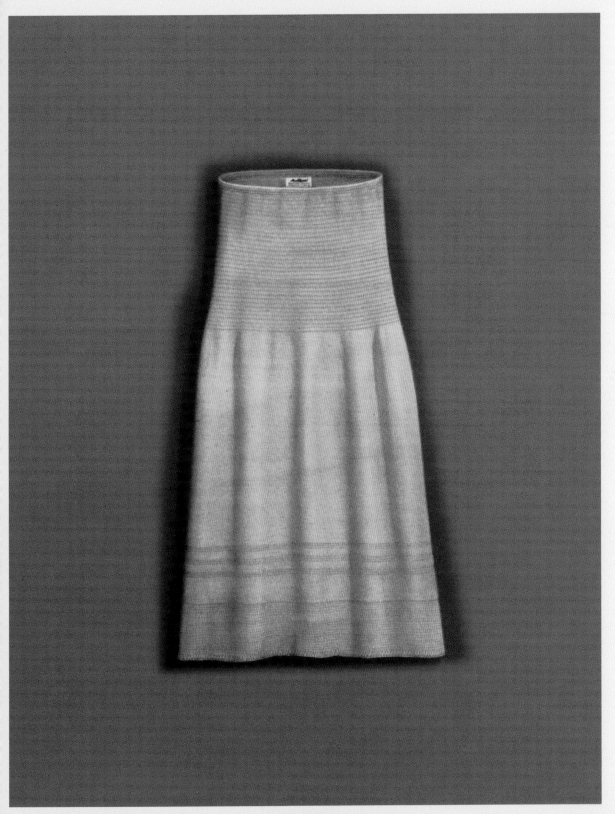

32 C 7405

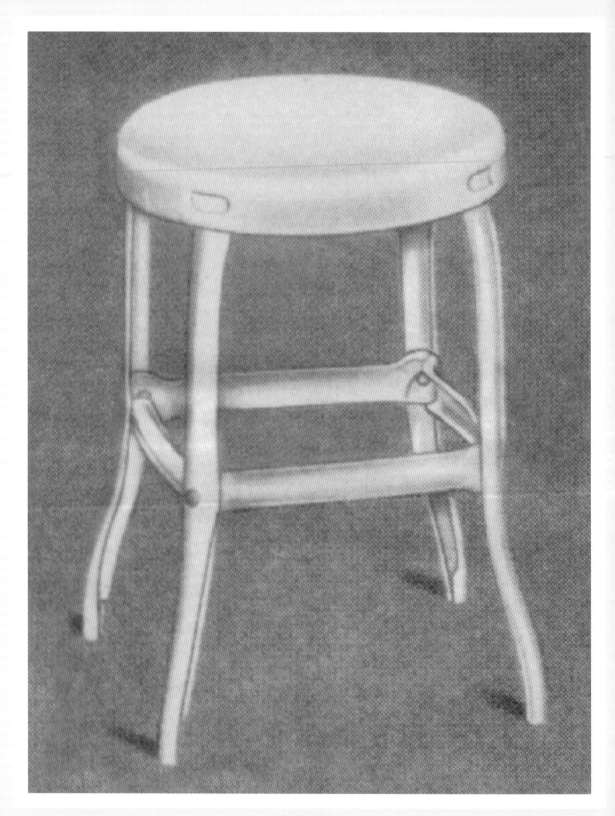

83 C 3097

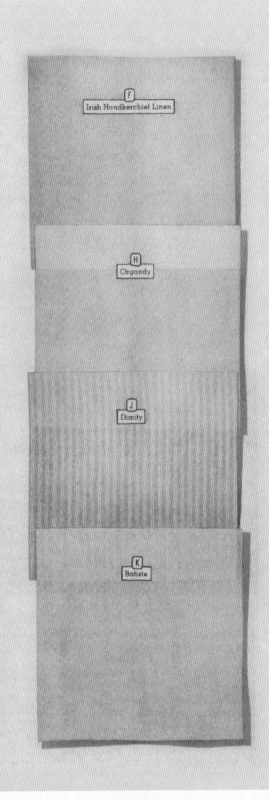

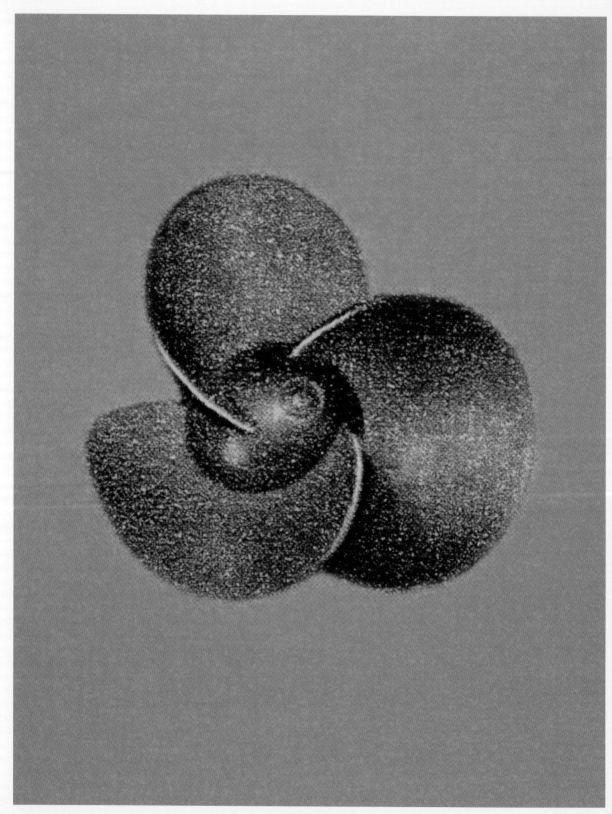

61 C 6040

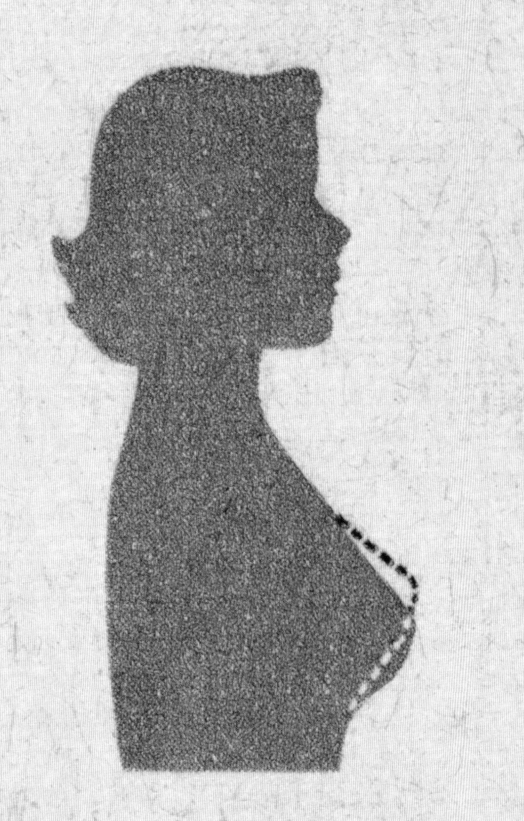

B CUP

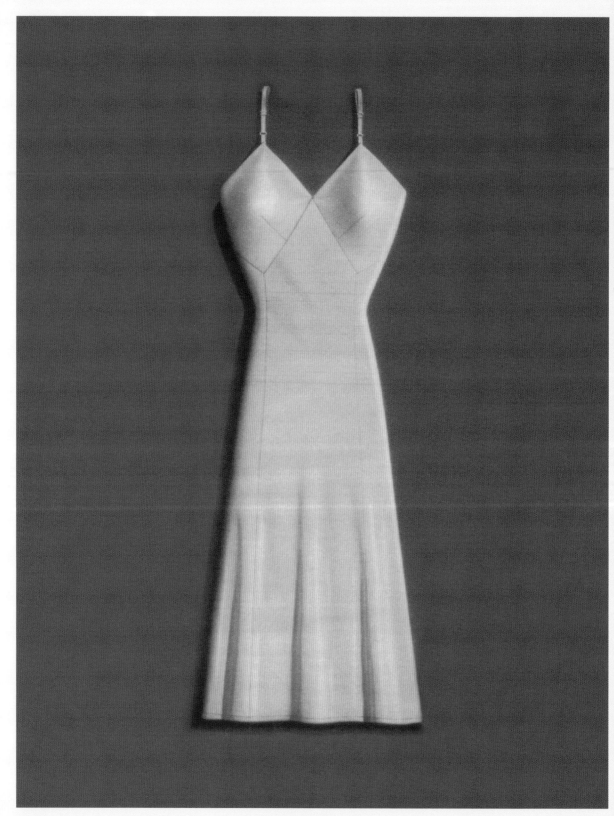

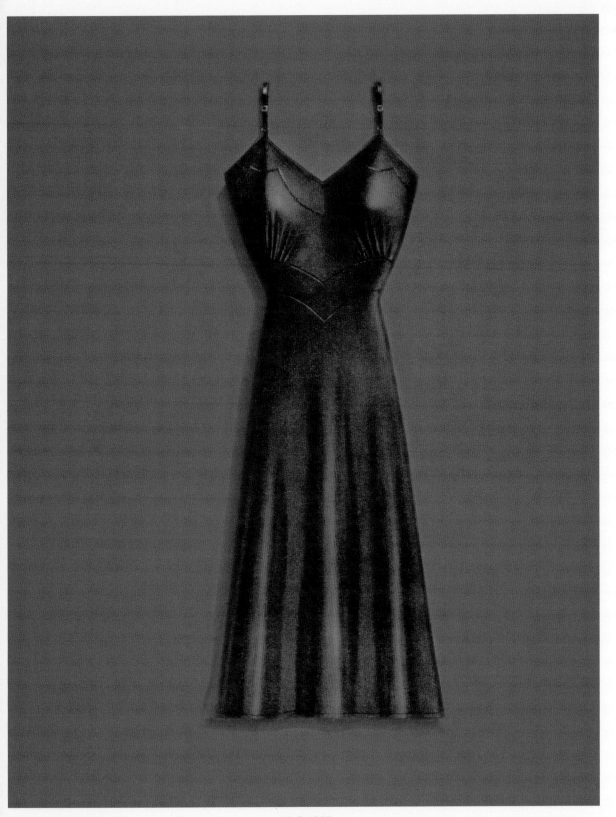

32 C 1037

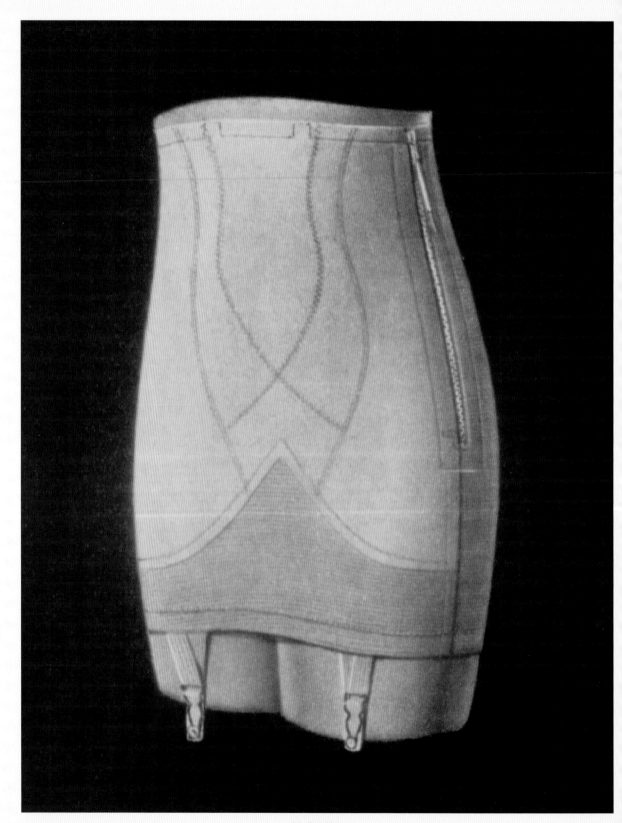

32 C 6290

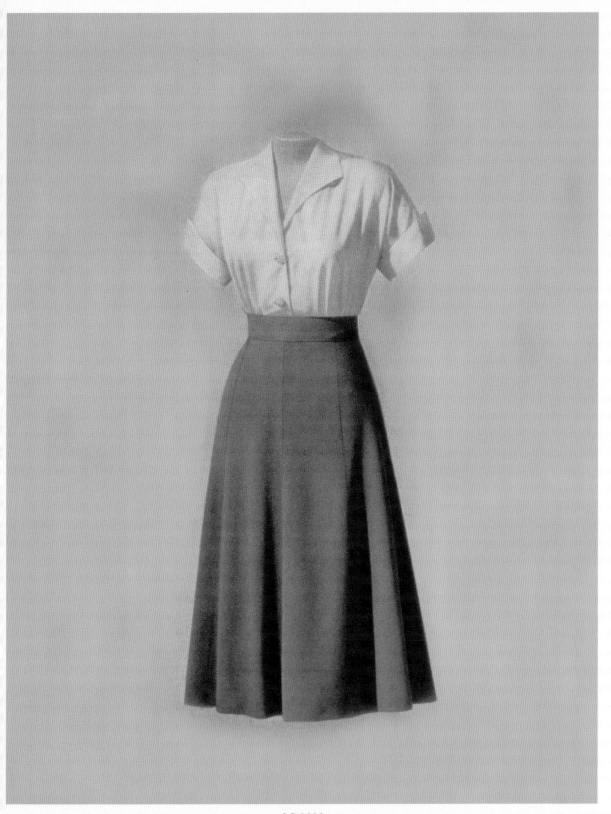

SC 1896

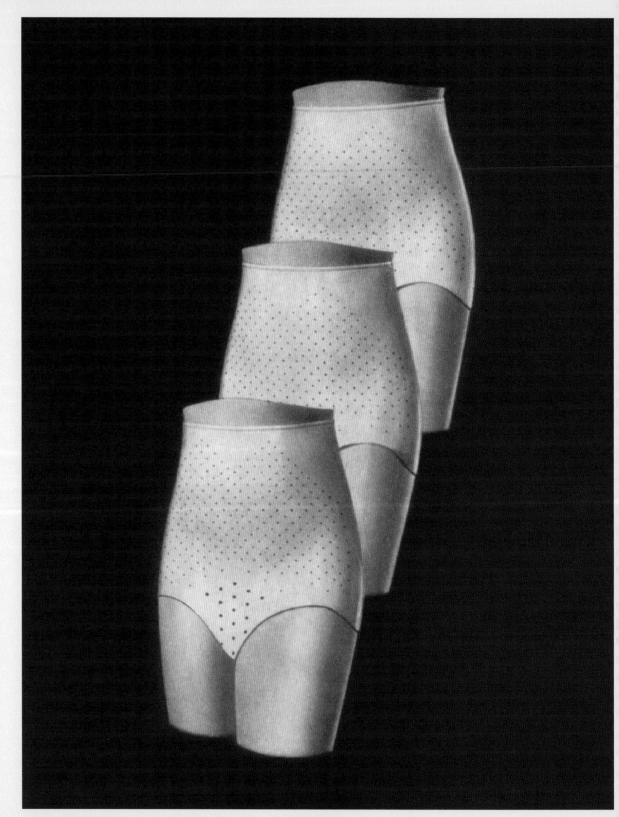

32 C 6471

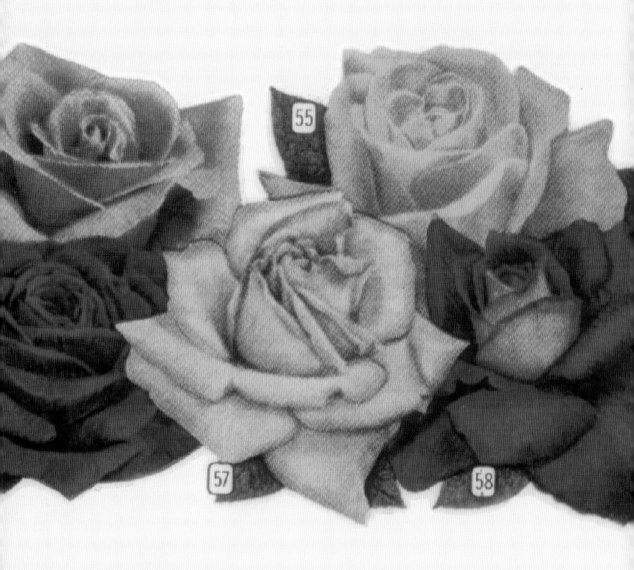

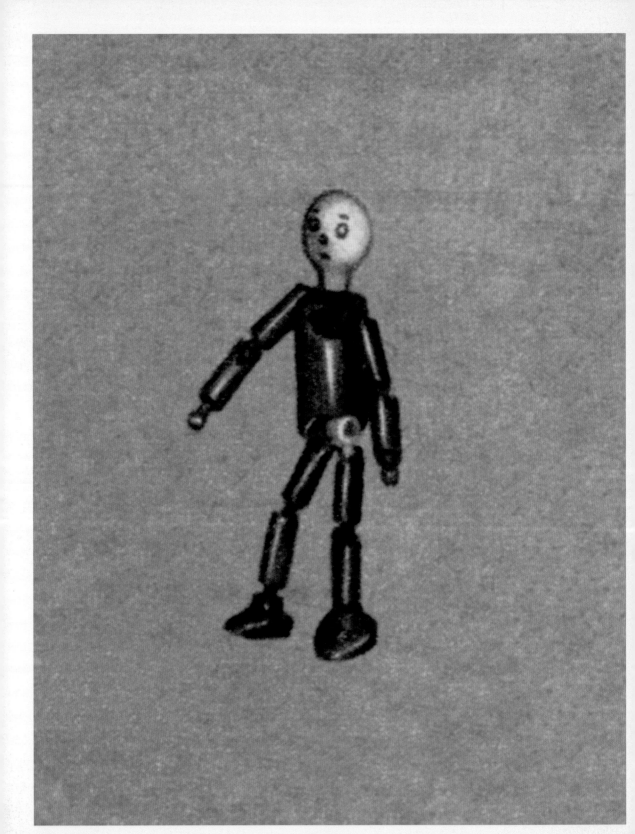

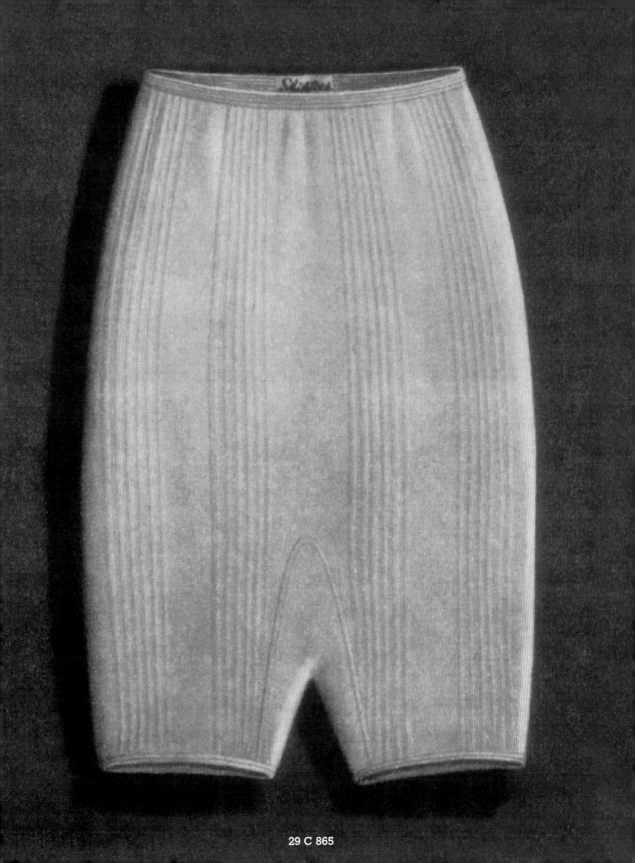

29 C 865

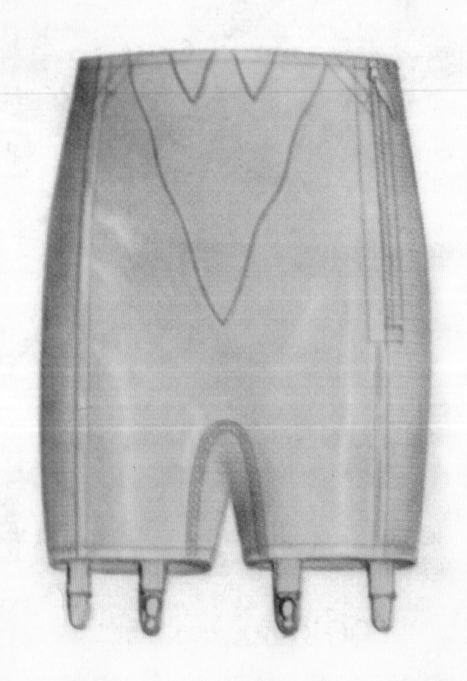

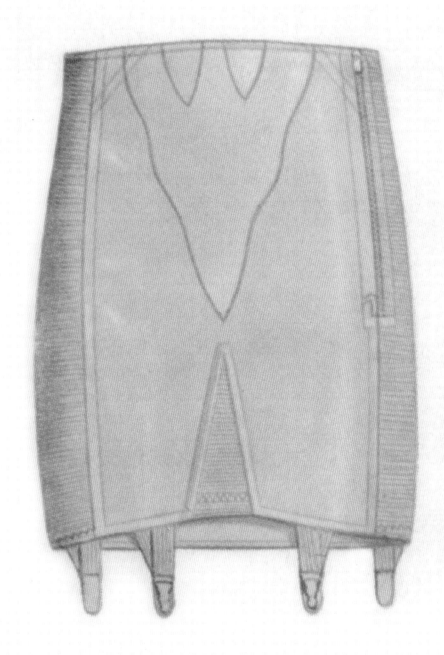

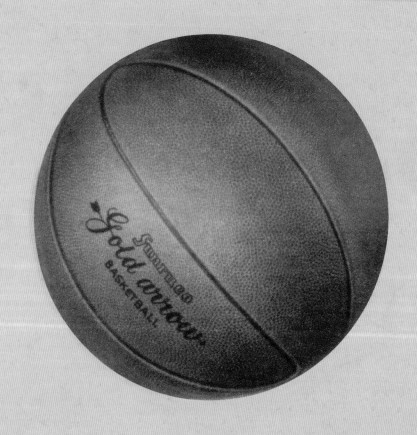

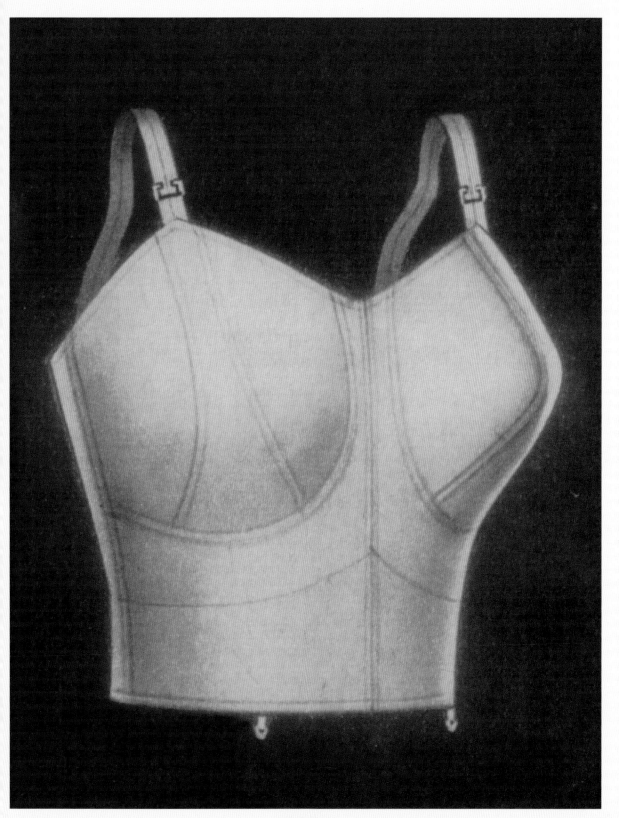

32 C 5011

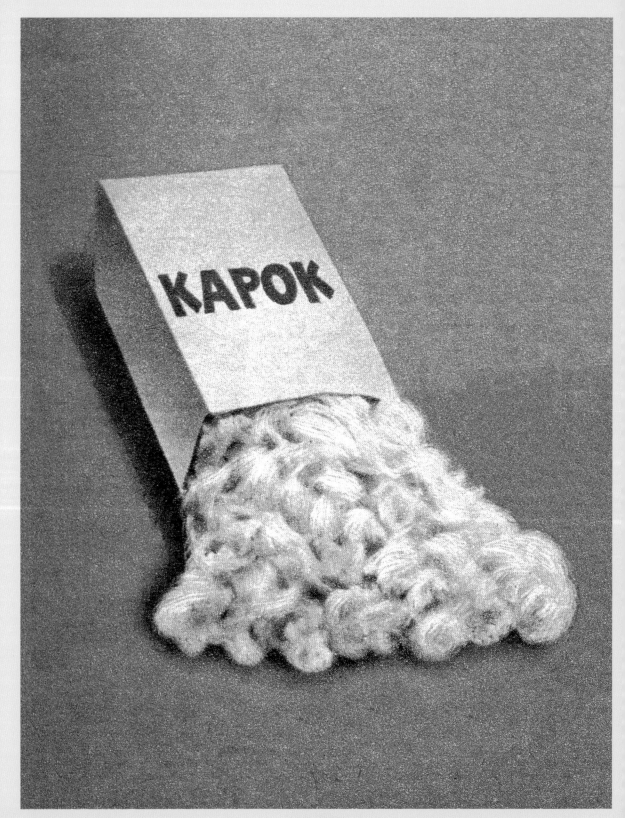

18 C 4580

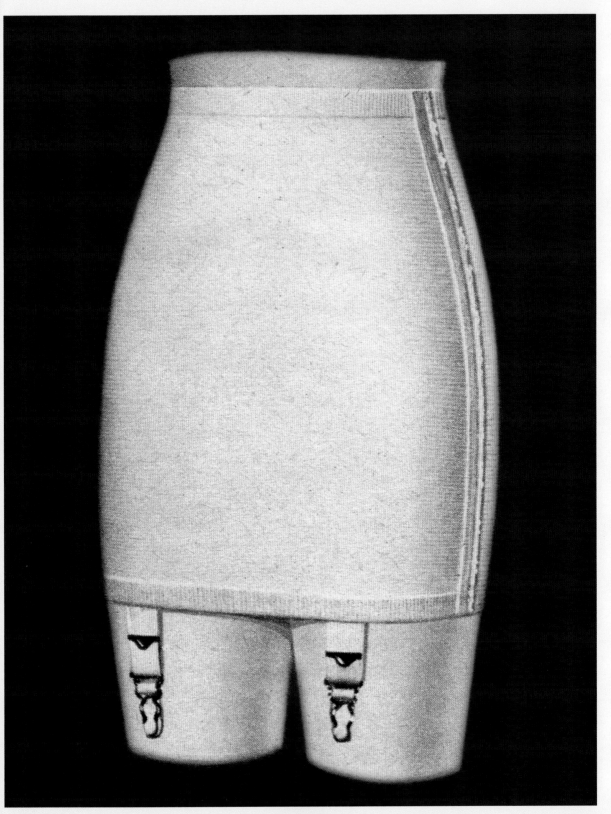

32C6225

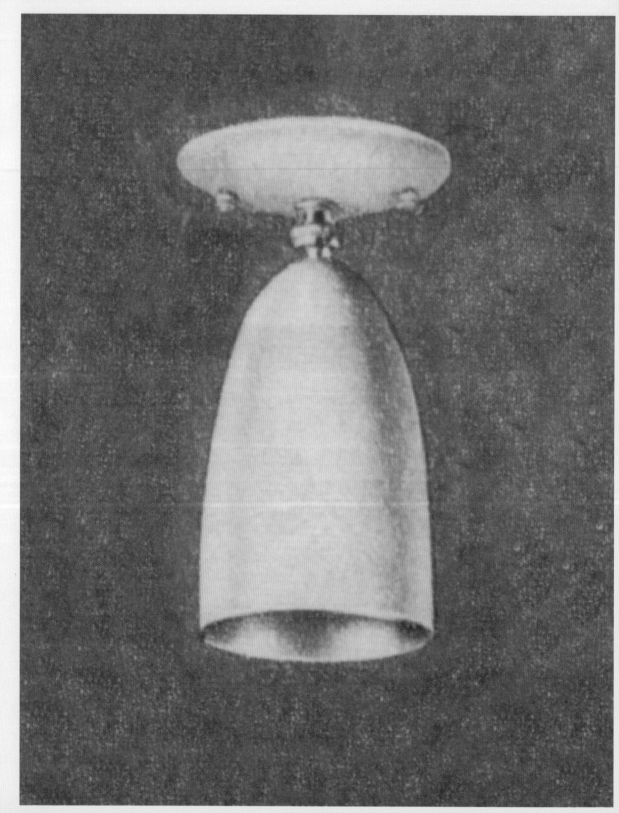

83 C 2526 L

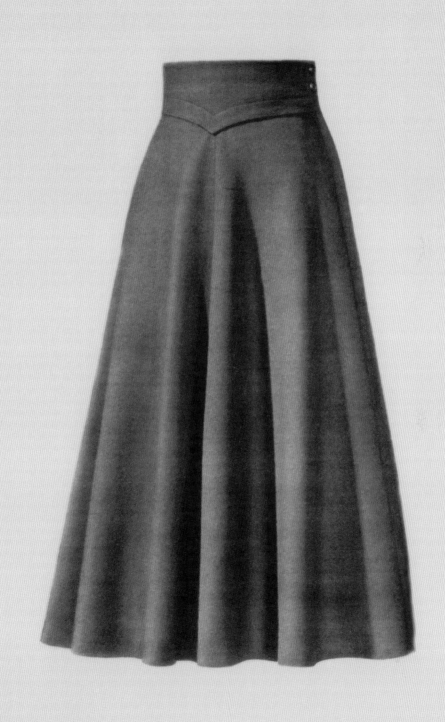

SC 1853

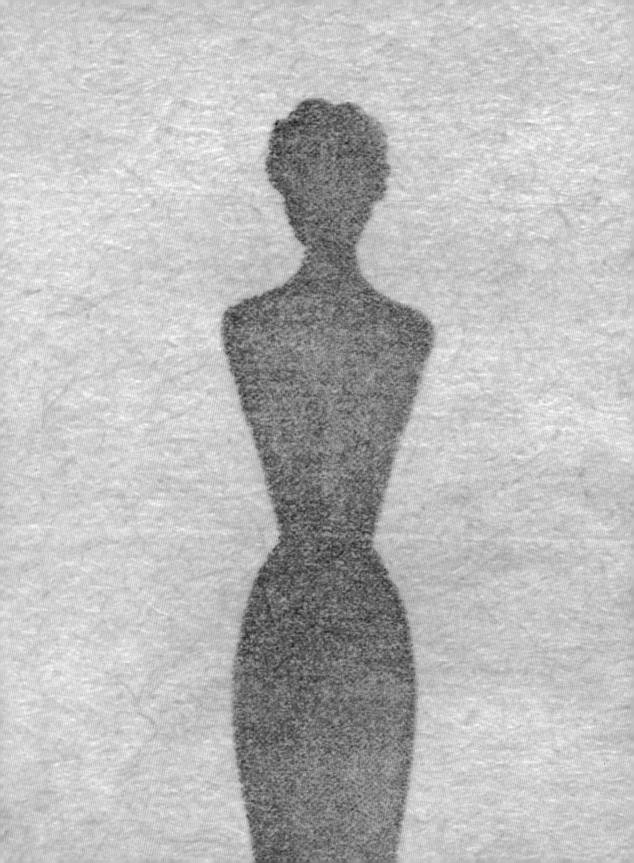

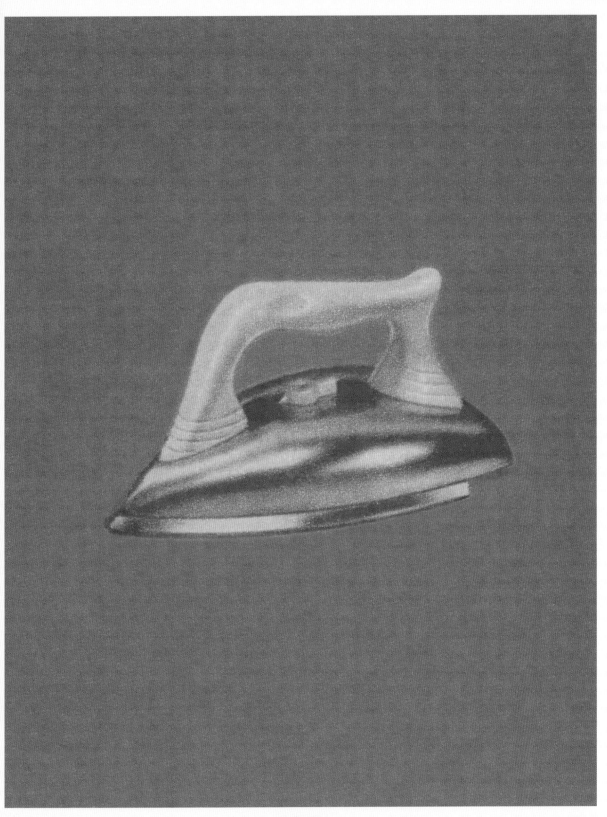

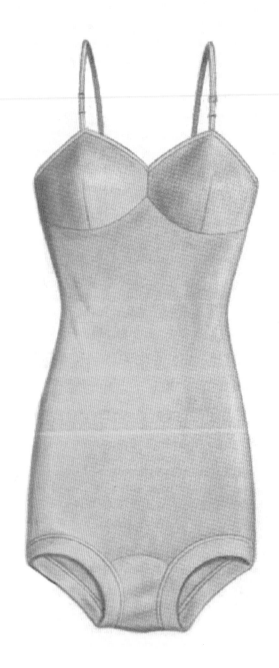

32 C 550

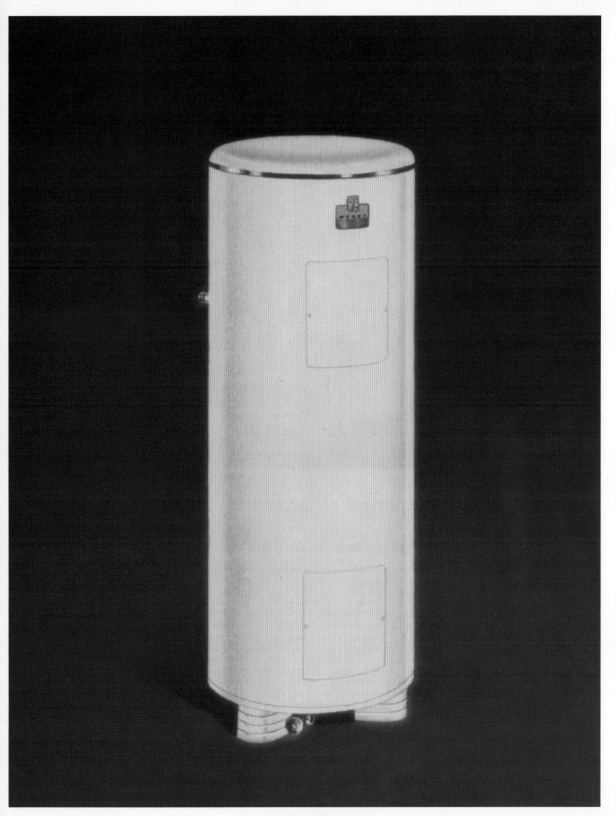

81 C 2860 R

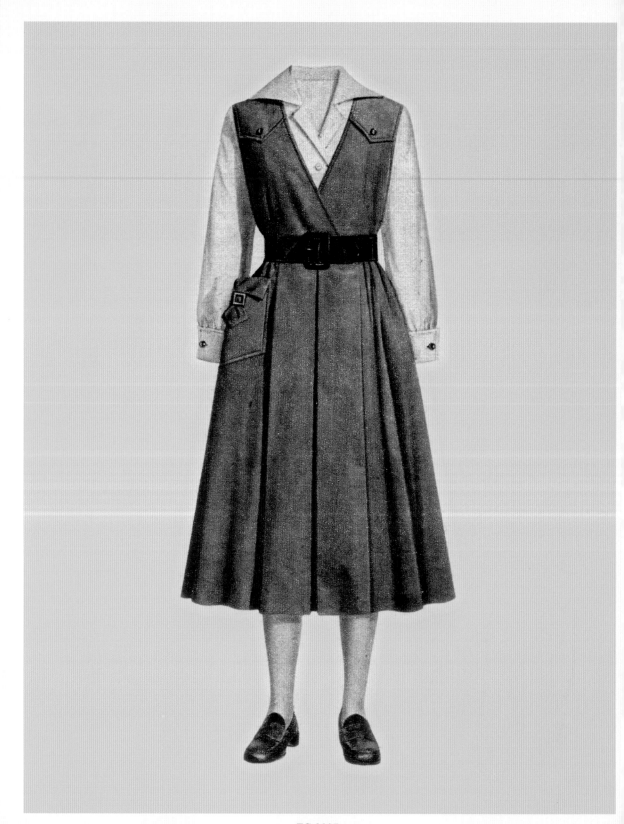

EC 3095

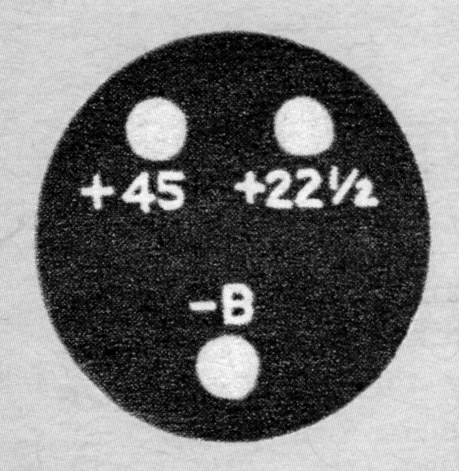

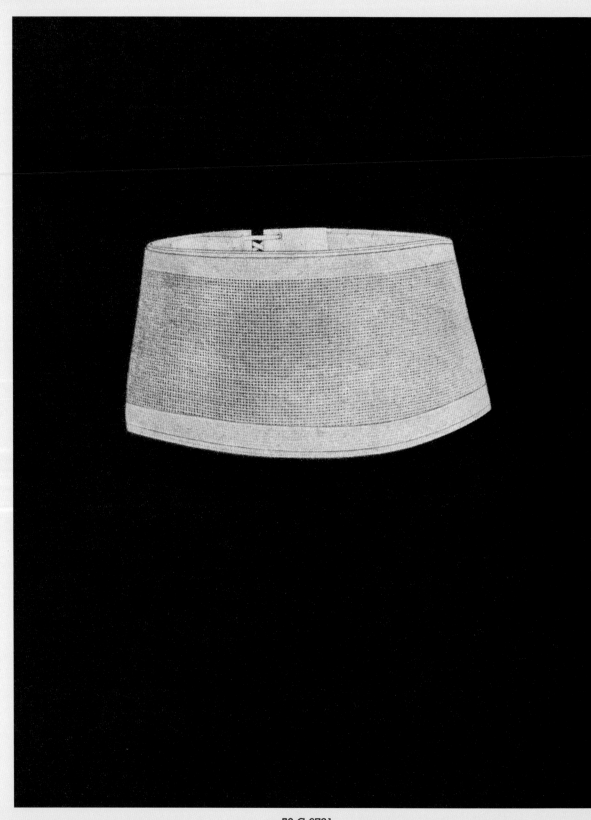

53 C 6731

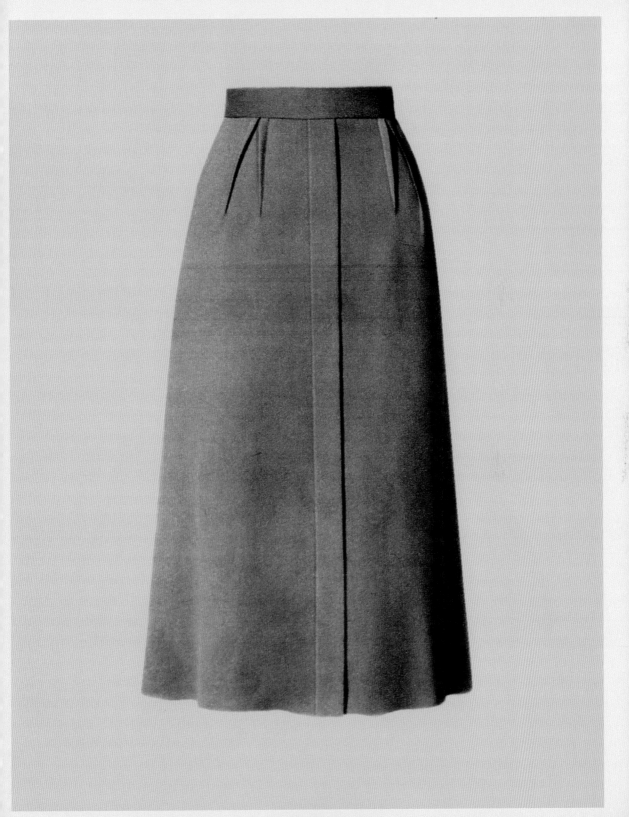

SC 1733

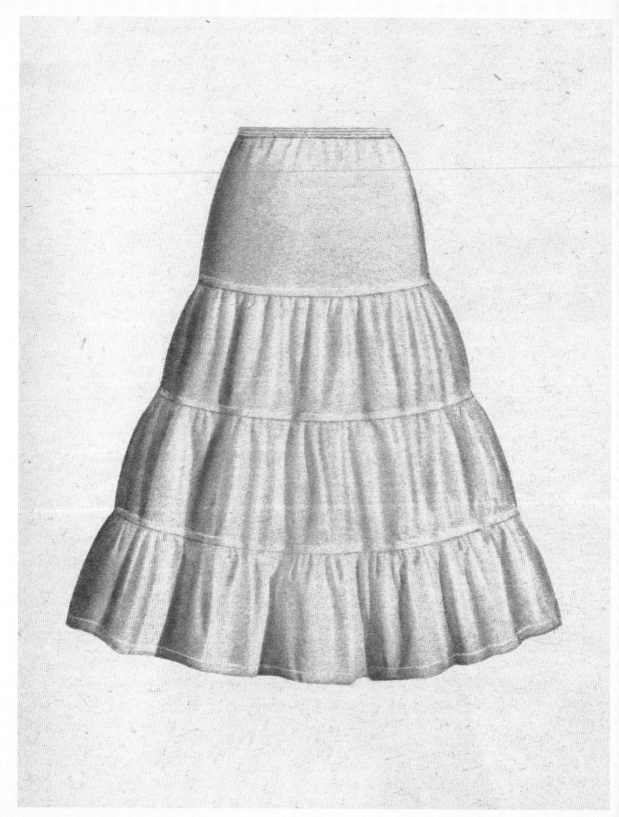

32C1997

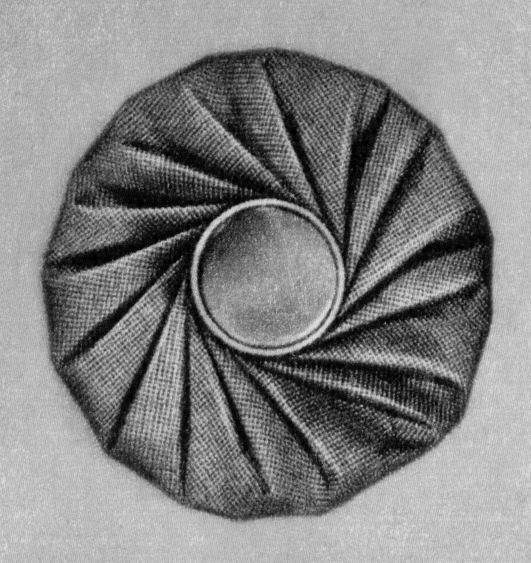

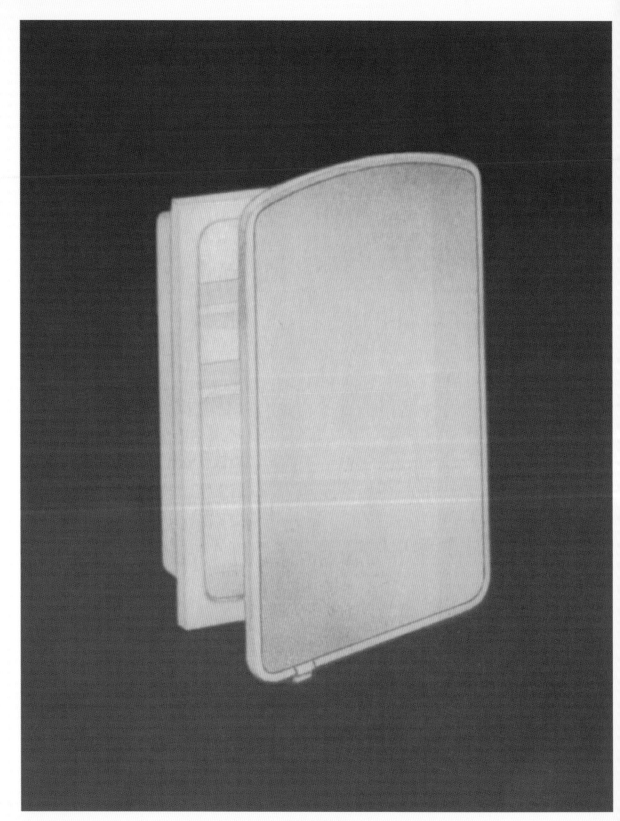

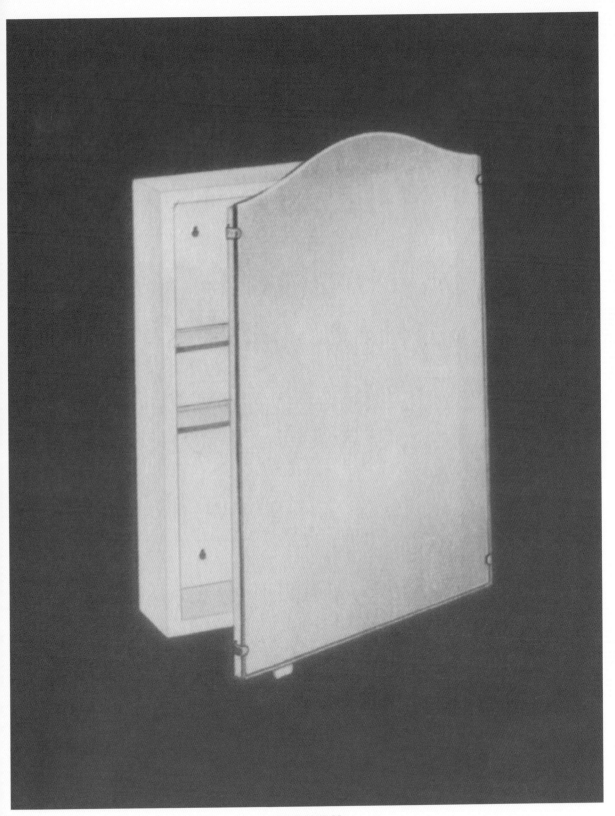

81 C 1155 M

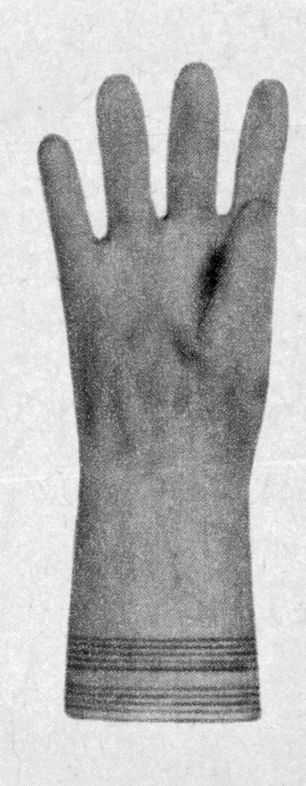

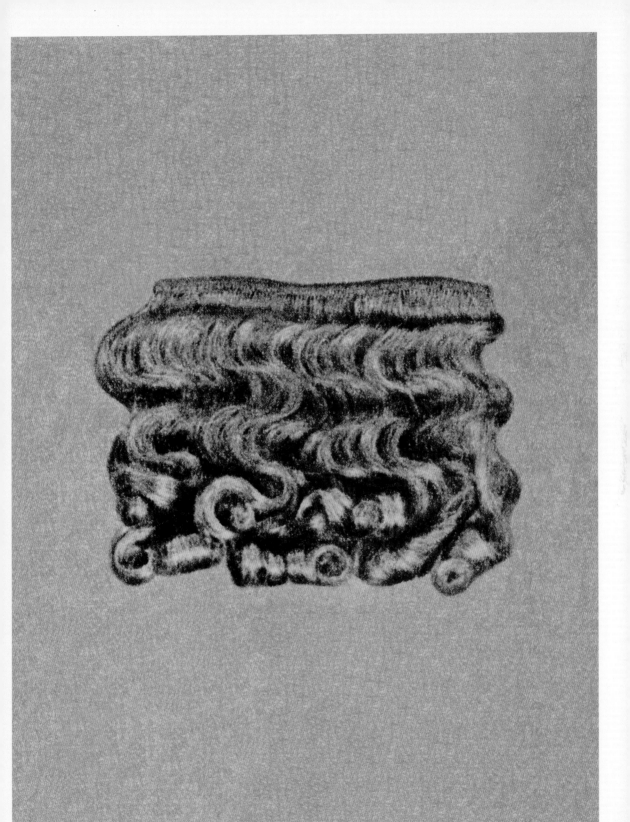

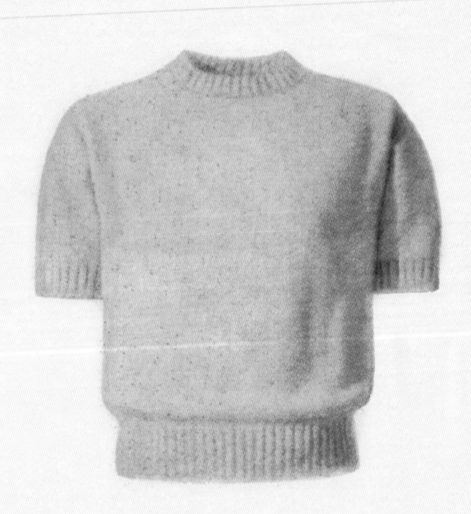

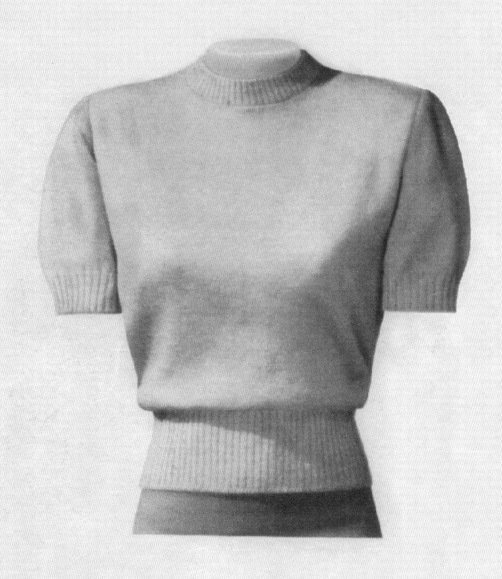

SC 4141

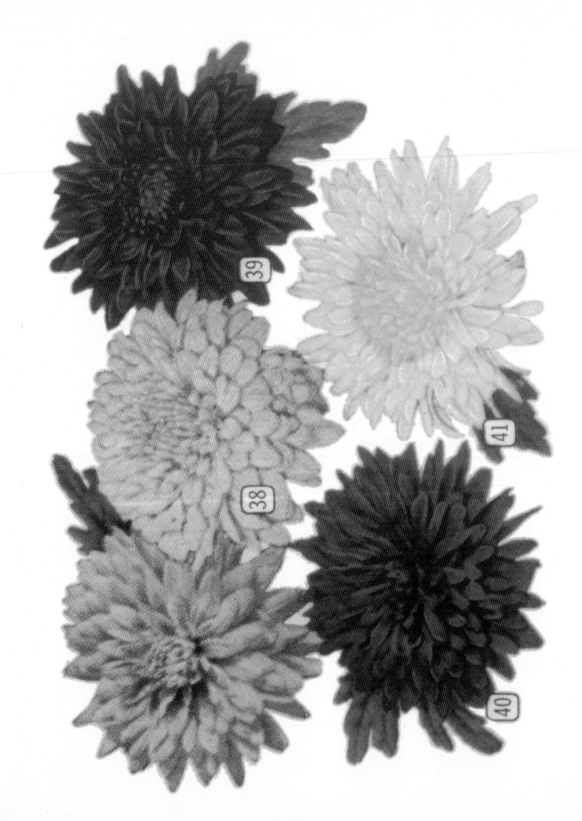

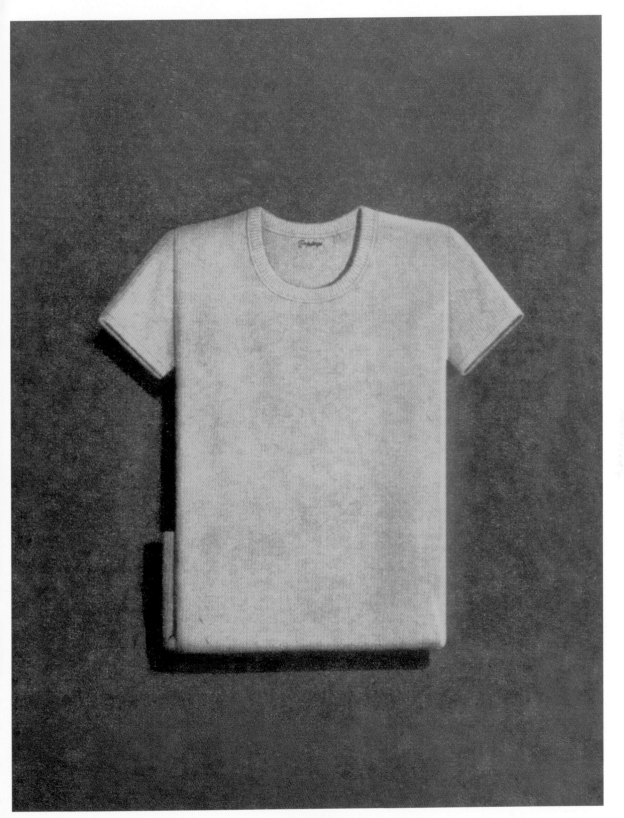

29 C 865

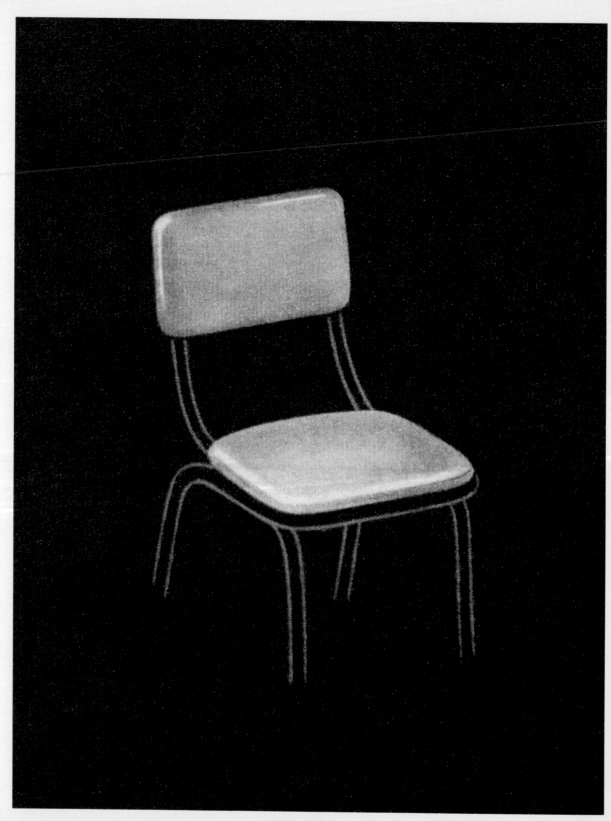

66 A 4126 M

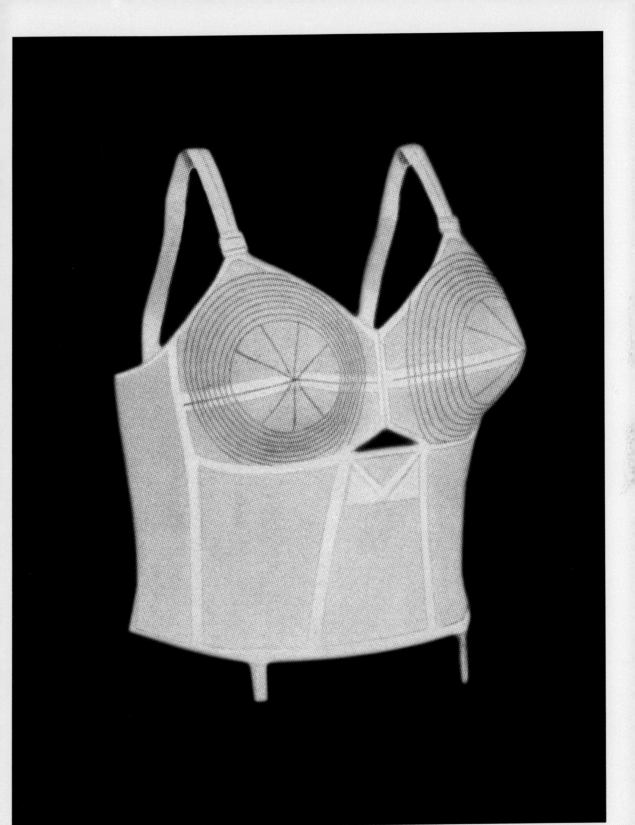

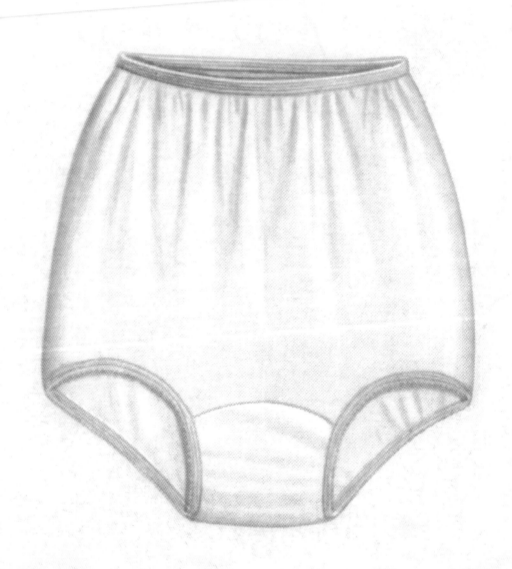

32 C 801

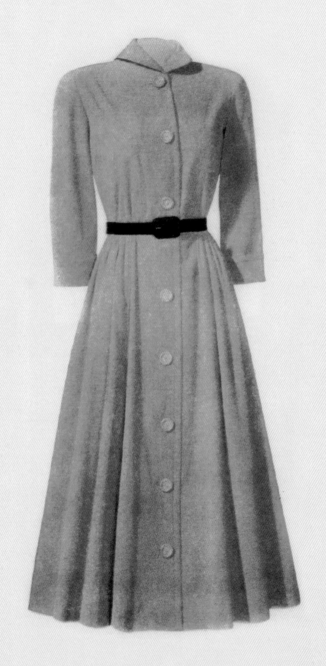

RC 5314

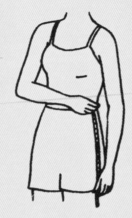

AUTHOR AND DESIGNER

CARIN GOLDBERG studied painting and graphic design at The Cooper Union School of Art. She began her career in graphic design 25 years ago in the CBS Television Network art department, went on to the advertising department at CBS Records (now Sony), and had a short stint designing album covers at Atlantic Records. Carin later moved to the CBS Records packaging department, where she designed covers for jazz, classical, and pop artists. In 1982, she left CBS and established Carin Goldberg Design. She continued to design covers for such artists as Madonna, the J. Geils Band, and the Wallflowers, and re-established a new look for the revamped Nonesuch Records. Carin has also designed hundreds of book jackets for numerous major publishers. For the past 18 years she has taught Typography and Senior Design Portfolio at the School of Visual Arts in New York City and has lectured on her career in major cities here and abroad. Carin's work has been consistently chosen in design competitions for the AIGA, the Art Director's Club, the Type Director's Club, and the Society of Publication Designers. Her work has been shown in the Walker Art Center's *Graphic Design in America* and the Cooper-Hewitt National Design Museum's *Mixing Messages*. She is the recipient of the silver medal from the Art Director's Club and has twice received publishing's Literary Marketplace Award. Carin is a recently elected member of AGI (*Alliance Graphique Internationale*). She currently lives in upstate New York with her husband James, son Julian, and extremely needy dog Lily.

INTRODUCTION

DOROTHY TWINING GLOBUS has been passionately involved with museums, exhibitions, design, and collecting for the past three decades. She has developed and presented more than 200 exhibitions exploring such aspects of design as architecture, graphics, decorative arts, fashion, and textiles. She served for seven years as Director of the Museum at the Fashion Institute of Technology and prior to that for 20 years as Curator of Exhibitions at the Cooper-Hewitt National Design Museum. She recently authored *Fashion-a la Mode, the Pop Up History of Costumes and Dresses* (Universe), and is currently working on independent projects as a curator and writer. Dorothy serves on the Board of Directors of the International Design Conference at Aspen, the Board of the Annette Green Fragrance Museum, and on the Trustees Council of the Preservation League of New York State.

ACKNOWLEDGMENTS

I would like to thank all of those who encouraged me to pursue this project. First and foremost I want to thank my editor Marisa Bulzone for her vision and enthusiasm and for making the process a creative and happy experience. I could not have pulled this together without my assistant Mary Belibasakis. Her patience and expertise were indispensible. Neil Flewellen for his love and friendship and daily belief in me. Gene Greif for his help and internet skills. Susan Hochbaum for her friendship (and sending me to Marisa). Akiko Busch for her ever-present encouragement. Kim Tyner and Galen Smith for their help in making this book shine. My students, past and present, for their inspiration and youthful energy. My husband James and son Julian for everything and more.

COPYRIGHT

THIS BOOK IS DEDICATED TO MY MOTHER, EDITH

ORDER BLANK

Complete satisfaction guaranteed or your money back

Date_____19___

How to Send Money: The safest and best ways to send money are: Postal Money Orders; Express Money Orders; Bank Money Orders or Bank Drafts; Cashier's Checks or your own Personal Check. For money order rates and other ways to send money, see preceding pages. If you live on a rural route, your mail carrier will buy a Postal Money Order for you on request.

Parcel Post Charges should be included with order. See preceding page for amount to send. Be sure to send enough to cover postage. *If you send too much we will refund every penny not needed.*
Freight or Express Charges should not be sent with order except when there is no agent at your station. To estimate them, see rates on preceding pages.

[1] **Name and Address** Please PRINT OR WRITE name and address plainly. All members of same household should order under one name.

Name_____
(First Name)   (Middle Initial)   (Last Name)

Street Address_____Route_____Box_____
(Please fill in completely whether needed for delivery or not)

Post Office_____State_____

[2] **How Shall We Ship:** ☐ Parcel Post ☐ Express ☐ Rail Freight ☐ Motor Truck

(Show Preferred Routing, if desired, on Rail or Truck Freight Orders only)

_____(Give your Freight Station here if different from your Post Office)
Do not send money for freight or express charges if there is an agent at your station.

[3] **Ship to Another Address** If you want this Order shipped to an address or person different from that given at left, write directions here:

Name_____
(First Name)   (Middle Initial)   (Last Name)

Street Address_____Route_____Box_____
(Please fill in completely whether needed for delivery or not)

Post Office_____State_____

[4] **If you have moved** since sending your last order, write old address here.

Street Address_____Route_____Box_____

Post Office_____State_____

Please do not write in this space

BE SURE TO STATE COLOR—PATTERN—FINISH ☞ ☜ **DON'T FORGET SIZE** See Measuring Instructions Given in Catalog

CATALOG NUMBER OF ARTICLE	Quantity Wanted	NAME OF ARTICLE—If to be initialed. Print initials below article ordered	COLOR Pattern, Finish, etc.	SIZE Width, etc.	PRICE Each, Yard Pair, etc.	TOTAL PRICE Dollars	Cents	SHIP. WTS. Lbs.	Oz.
			COLOR	SIZE					
			COLOR	SIZE					
			COLOR	SIZE					
			COLOR	SIZE					
			COLOR	SIZE					
			COLOR	SIZE					
			COLOR	SIZE					
			COLOR	SIZE					
			COLOR	SIZE					
			COLOR	SIZE					
			COLOR	SIZE				Pounds	Ounces

PLEASE do Not Write Here
Total Received

Credit on other part

Credit on this part

Tax Notice We are required by law to pay tax on sales in New York City, Maine, Rhode Island and Connecticut.
If you live in New York City, add 3% (3 cents on the dollar) to the amount of your order for tax.
If you live in Maine or Rhode Island, add 2% (2 cents on the dollar) to the amount of your order for tax.
In Connecticut there is a tax of 2% (2 cents on the dollar) on any item priced over $25—except Children's Wear, on which there is no tax. If you live in Connecticut, add 2% to the amount of your order for each item over $25 requiring this tax.

If this is a CASH ORDER Check Here ☐
and enclose remittance in full, including postage and tax.

If a MONTHLY PAYMENT ORDER Check Here ☐
and fill-in and sign the form on other side

	Dollars	Cents
TOTAL FOR GOODS		
AMOUNT FOR TAX (If any—Notice at left)		
POSTAGE (We refund any not used)		
AMOUNT I OWE (if any) from Previous Order		
AMOUNT ENCLOSED		

Total Wt. in Lbs. | A

CAUTION· Always give the complete Catalog Number of each article (Example 86 C 174M), not just the little letter or number that identifies the illustration.